PRAYER & STUDY GUIDE

The Power of a

PRAYING®

Parent

STORMIE
OMARTIAN

HARVEST HOUSE PUBLISHERS
EUGENE, OREGON

Scripture quotations are taken from the New King James Version. Copyright © 1982 by Thomas Nelson, Inc. Used by permission. All rights reserved.

Cover by Harvest House Publishers, Inc., Eugene, Oregon

Cover illustration © Komar art / Shutterstock

Back cover photo © Michael Gomez Photography

THE POWER OF A PRAYING is a registered trademark of The Hawkins Children's LLC. Harvest House Publishers, Inc., is the exclusive licensee of the federally registered trademark THE POWER OF A PRAYING.

THE POWER OF A PRAYING® PARENT PRAYER AND STUDY GUIDE
Copyright © 2000, 2014 by Stormie Omartian
Published by Harvest House Publishers
Eugene, Oregon 97402
www.harvesthousepublishers.com

ISBN 978-0-7369-5773-1 (pbk.)
ISBN 978-0-7369-5775-5 (eBook)

Printed in the United States of America

18 19 20 21 22 / BP-CD / 10 9 8 7 6 5 4

A supplemental workbook to
The Power of a Praying® Parent
by Stormie Omartian
for those interested in practical
group or individual study.

Contents

How Do I Begin?

Welcome to the wonderful and fulfilling task of becoming an effective praying parent. While it is easy for every mom and dad to have the desire to pray for their child, knowing *how* to pray specifically can often be a challenge. That's because each child is unique. What works for one may not work for another. And with each age, there are new challenges and concerns. At one point they are too young to tell you what is going on in their lives, at another they don't *want* to tell you what is going on in their lives. And once they reach adulthood, you never really know what is going on in their lives. Prayer is the only solution. The good news is that God has given you the authority to intercede powerfully for your child no matter what age he (she) is or whether he (she) lives with you or not. And He will give you the revelation you need to pray on target. This workbook is intended to assist you in that.

What You'll Need

This *Prayer and Study Guide* is divided into a 31-week plan for use in personal or group study. You will need to have my book *The Power of a Praying Parent* to read along with this. The answers to many of the questions will be found in it. You will also need a Bible. I have quoted the New King James Version here, but you can use whatever translation you want. Just make sure the Bible you have is easy for you to understand, and one you feel free to write in.

About Your Answers

Many of the questions in this *Prayer and Study Guide* will have to be answered separately for each individual child. If you are praying for more than one child, you will not have room in this book for all of your answers. In that case, it would be beneficial to keep your responses in a notebook or journal. The answers are not for anyone else to read, and you will not be tested on them. They are to help you determine how to pray specifically for each child. This kind of prayer notebook for your children is wonderful to keep and look back on years later. You will be amazed at how strategically the Lord directed you to pray and how He answered those prayers.

Try to answer all the questions and follow the directions to the best of your ability. Even if your child is an infant, or he (she) is grown and has been gone from your home for some time, God will reveal things to you about him (her) with regard to the questions. Try to write something for each entry. If nothing else, write what is in your heart regarding that question. When instructed to write out a prayer, it doesn't have to be a lengthy one. Two or three sentences will cover the subject of focus.

How to Proceed

In group study, it's good to follow the order of this book so that everyone will literally be on the same page when they come together each week. In individual study, you do not have to proceed in the same order if there are more pressing concerns that need to be addressed immediately. In any case, however, Chapter One and Chapter Two of *The Power of a Praying Parent* should be read before proceeding on to any others.

In a Group

When studying in a group, read the appropriate chapter in *The Power of a Praying Parent* and answer the questions in the corresponding chapter here in the *Prayer and Study Guide* on your own.

When the group comes together, the leader will go over the questions and discuss what insights God has given each person as he or she feels led to share them. This will be the perfect time to pray as a group for your children. Group intercession for children is very powerful, so take advantage of every opportunity to pray for them in this way.

How to Pray a Scripture

Frequently you will be asked to write out a specific scripture as a prayer over yourself or your child. This is to help you learn to include the Word of God in your prayers. Also, there is power in writing out your prayers. To help you understand how to do that, I have included an example of how I pray Ephesians 6:10-11 over my daughter. Look it up in your Bible and see how I have personalized it:

> "I pray that Mandy will be strong in You, Lord, and move in Your power. I pray that she will be able to put on the whole armor of God. I pray that Mandy will be able to stand strong against the wiles of the devil."

Your Role

Your role is to become an intercessor for your child. *An intercessor is one who prays for someone and makes possible the ability of that person to better hear from God.* No one else on earth will ever pray for your child with the fervency and consistency that you will. What an awesome opportunity to powerfully affect your child's life for eternity.

WEEK ONE

Read Chapter 1: "Becoming a Praying Parent"
from *The Power of a Praying Parent*

1. List three traits you see as your child's best qualities.

_____

_____

_____

_____

_____

_____

2. How could these good qualities become liabilities if they are not
   covered in prayer?

_____

_____

_____

_____

_____

_____

3. List the three biggest concerns you have for your child.

_____

_____

_____

_____

_____

_____

4. Do you ever feel overwhelmed by any of these concerns? _____.
    In what way?

_____

_____

_____

_____

_____

_____

5. Does your child have any negative character traits that need to
    be covered in prayer? _____. What are they?

_____

_____

_____

_____

_____

_____

6. How could these negative traits be turned into positive qualities or assets in your child's life? (For example, a child's tendency to dominate other children could be tempered by the love of God, mixed with a heart of compassion, and turned into a great leadership quality.)

_____

_____

_____

_____

_____

_____

7. Look up James 4:7 and underline it in your Bible. Who are you supposed to resist? _____. When you resist, what will happen? _____. Do you believe that you can successfully resist the enemy's plans for your children in prayer? _____. Why or why not?

_____

_____

_____

_____

_____

_____

8. Read Deuteronomy 32:30 and underline it in your Bible. According to this, how many of the enemy's forces can you cause to flee when you pray? _____. How many when you pray with one other person? _____. Do you believe there is power in praying with other believers for your children? _____. Why or why not?

_____

_____

_____

_____

_____

9. In what ways do you feel you have done a good job as a parent?

_____

_____

_____

_____

_____

10. Do you feel you have ever made any mistakes as a parent? _____. If so, list what they are and what would you have done differently. Write out your answer as a prayer asking God to redeem those situations.

_____

_____

_____

_____

11. Do you ever feel guilt as a parent? _____. Why or why not? (All parents at one time or another feel guilt about something regarding their children. The purpose of this question is not to make you feel bad, but rather to identify this area so that the devil can't use it against you.)

_____

_____

_____

_____

12. Is there anything you would like to change about yourself or your life that would alleviate the guilt you feel as a parent? Write out your answer as a prayer asking God to help you make those changes.

_____

_____

_____

_____

_____

13. Do you feel that you generally expect a lot of yourself as a parent? _____. Do you expect yourself to be a perfect parent? _____. Explain your answers.

_____

_____

_____

_____

14. Read Romans 8:1 and underline it in your Bible. How are we to walk in order to be free of feeling condemnation? _____ _____. How are we not to walk? _____ _____. Write out a prayer asking God to help you walk free of condemnation.

_____

_____

_____

_____

15. Read Ephesians 6:12-13 and underline these verses in your Bible. Whom are we wrestling against when we pray? _____ _____. What are we supposed to do to withstand them? _____ _____. Write out a prayer asking God to help you do that, especially with regard to your children.

_____

_____

_____

_____

16. Read 1 Peter 5:8-9 and underline these verses in your Bible. Who is your enemy and the enemy of your children? _____ _____. What is he constantly doing? _____. What are you to do in response?

_____

_____

_____

_____

17. Read Luke 10:19 and underline it in your Bible. God has given you authority over all _____. That means for your children as well as yourself. Do you ever see the enemy trying to threaten your child in any way? _____. If so, in what way?

    _____

    _____

    _____

    _____

18. Read John 15:5 and underline it in your Bible. How does this verse apply to you as a parent? _____ _____. Are you able to fully depend on God to help you raise your children? Write out your answer as a prayer telling God what you need in that regard.

    _____

    _____

    _____

    _____

19. Read 1 Peter 4:8. What will cover the places where we miss the mark as parents? _____. Write out a prayer asking God to help you love your child with such unconditional love that it smooths all the rough places, heals all wounds, and covers your weaknesses.

    _____

    _____

    _____

20. Pray out loud the prayer on page 28 in *The Power of a Praying Parent*. Include any specifics about yourself as a parent.

_____

_____

_____

_____

WEEK TWO

Read Chapter 2: "Releasing My Child into God's
Hands" from *The Power of a Praying Parent*

1. Are you highly protective of your child to the point that you
   constantly worry over his (her) safety? _____. Explain
   why or why not.

   _____

   _____

   _____

   _____

   _____

2. Read 1 Peter 5:6-7 and underline these verses in your Bible.
   What are you supposed to do with your cares and concerns for
   your child? _____. Are you able to eas-
   ily do that?

   _____

   _____

   _____

   _____

   _____

3. Do you believe God is a good Father and that He loves your child even more than you do? _____. Explain why you do or do not believe that.

_____

_____

_____

_____

_____

4. Have you asked God to be in control of your life? _____. Of your child's life? _____. Why or why not?

_____

_____

_____

_____

_____

5. Where does prayer for your child begin? _____.

Releasing your child into God's hands is a sign of _____ _____. (See page 33, last paragraph, in *The Power of a Praying Parent*.)

_____

_____

_____

_____

_____

6. Do you believe that when you release your child to God, (she) will be in good hands? _____. Why or why no

   _____

   _____

   _____

   _____

   _____

7. Is there any reason why it would be difficult for you to fully release your child into God's hands? _____.
   Explain your answer.

   _____

   _____

   _____

   _____

   _____

8. Read Isaiah 65:23 and underline it in your Bible. Put a star next to it. Write it out below as a proclamation and claim it as a promise for your child. For example, "I do not labor in vain. I did not bring forth (<u>name of child</u>) for trouble..."

   _____

   _____

   _____

   _____

   _____

). Read Psalm 127:3 and underline it in your Bible. Do you believe your child is a blessing from God? _____. Why or why not?

_____

_____

_____

_____

_____

10. Pray out loud the prayer on page 34 in *The Power of a Praying Parent*. Include specifics God has revealed about you or your child.

_____

_____

_____

_____

_____

WEEK THREE

Read Chapter 3: "Securing Protection from Harm"
from *The Power of a Praying Parent*

1. What are the greatest dangers that most concern you for your child?

   _____

   _____

   _____

   _____

2. Write out a prayer asking God to protect your child specifically from those things which most concern you.

   _____

   _____

   _____

3. Do you believe that God can protect your child from those dangers? _____. Why or why not?

   _____

   _____

   _____

4. Read Psalm 112:1-8 and underline these verses in your Bible. What does God promise to those who reverence and obey Him?

_____

_____

_____

_____

5. According to Psalm 112:1, are you the kind of person who is a candidate for God's blessings? _____. Why or why not?

_____

_____

_____

6. Does your child ever express fear for his (her) own safety? _____. Do you believe this is a valid fear? _____. Why or why not? How could you pray with and for your child concerning this fear?

_____

_____

_____

7. Write out a prayer asking God to reveal to you any hidden dangers that you do not see. When He shows them to you, write them down and add them to your prayer list for your child.

_____

_____

_____

8. Write out a prayer asking God to show you ~~~ you need
    to do to increase your child's safety. Then ask~~g
    peace about it.   ~~ give you

    _____

    _____

    _____

    _____

    _____

9. Read Psalm 61:1-5 and underline it in your Bible. Put a star next
    to verses 3 and 4. Write out these two verses as a prayer over your
    child. "Lord, I pray You will be a shelter for (name of child)..."

    _____

    _____

    _____

    _____

    _____

10. Pray out loud the prayer on page 41 in *The Power of a Praying
    Parent*. Include specifics about the protection of your child.

    _____

    _____

    _____

    _____

    _____

WEEK FOUR

Read Chapter 4: "Feeling Loved and Accepted"
from *The Power of a Praying Parent*

1. Read Isaiah 41:9-10 and underline these verses in your Bible.
   Do you believe that you are chosen and accepted by God?
   _____. Do you believe God will strengthen, help, and
   uphold you? _____. Why or why not?

   _____

   _____

   _____

   _____

   _____

2. Do you believe Isaiah 41:9-10 is true for your child? _____.
   Write out a prayer asking God to help your child believe that
   he (she) is chosen by God and that God will always be with him
   (her).

   _____

   _____

   _____

   _____

   _____

3. Descri'   v much you love your child.

_____

_____

_____

_____

_____

4. Have you told your child how much you love him (her)?
   _____. Are you certain your child perceives and believes
   that you love him (her) the way you say you do? _____.
   Explain.

_____

_____

_____

_____

_____

5. Did you feel loved as a child? _____. Do you think
   your experiences as a child have influenced the way you show
   love to your child? _____. How so?

_____

_____

_____

_____

_____

6. What can you do for your child today that will make him (her) feel loved? (If you don't know, ask God to show you and ask your child to tell you.)

   _____

   _____

   _____

   _____

   _____

7. Does your child generally feel accepted or rejected by people outside the family? _____. If you don't know, ask God to reveal that to you and ask your child to tell you. How could you pray about that?

   _____

   _____

   _____

   _____

8. Are there specific or isolated situations in your child's life when he (she) feels rejection? _____. Do you think this is a real concern, or has your child believed something that has no basis in truth? _____.
   How could you pray specifically about that?

   _____

   _____

   _____

   _____

9. Do you believe your child ever fears being rejected in certain
    social situations? _____. Write out a
    prayer which you could pray over your child whenever he (she)
    is about to enter an uncomfortable social situation.

    _____

    _____

    _____

    _____

    _____

10. Pray out loud the prayer on page 46 in *The Power of a Praying
    Parent.* Include specifics related to you and your child.

    _____

    _____

    _____

    _____

    _____

WEEK FIVE

Read Chapter 5: "Establishing an Eternal Future"
from *The Power of a Praying Parent*

1. Read John 6:40 and underline it in your Bible. Do you believe what Jesus says here is true? _____. In light of this verse, what is the most important thing you can pray about for your child?

   _____

   _____

   _____

   _____

   _____

2. Has your child received Jesus as his (her) Savior? _____.
   If not, write out a prayer about that. If yes, write out a prayer asking for his (her) relationship to grow deeper.

   _____

   _____

   _____

   _____

   _____

3. How would you describe your relationship with God? _____
   _____.
   How do you think that affects your child's relationship with
   God? _____
   _____. How could you
   pray about that?

   _____

   _____

   _____

   _____

4. Are you able to talk freely with your child about your relationship with God? _____. What is his (her) response?

   _____

   _____

   _____

   _____

   _____

5. Does your child talk openly and freely with you and others
   about his (her) relationship with God? _____. How could
   you pray about that?

   _____

   _____

   _____

   _____

6. Read John 14:12-14 and underline these verses in your Bible. Put a star next to verse 14. What does this verse mean to you?

_____

_____

_____

_____

_____

7. What is the promise in verse 14 for your child if he (she) believes in Jesus? _____

_____. Does your child understand and believe this?

_____

_____

_____

_____

8. Is there anything you could tell your child about the Lord's goodness to you that would inspire him (her) to draw closer to God or to love God more? Write it here, and then tell him (her) at your first opportunity.

_____

_____

_____

_____

9. According to page 51, last paragraph, in *The Power of a Praying Parent*, what should be a parent's ongoing prayer? Write that out as a prayer below. For example, "Lord, I pray that my child will always be filled with…"

_____

_____

_____

_____

_____

10. Pray out loud the prayer on page 52 in *The Power of a Praying Parent*. Include specifics that relate to your child.

_____

_____

_____

_____

_____

WEEK SIX

Read Chapter 6:
"Honoring Parents and Resisting Rebellion"
from *The Power of a Praying Parent*

1. Read Ephesians 6:1-3 and underline it in your Bible. In light of these verses, why is it important for you to teach your child to honor you as his or her parent? What could happen if you don't?

   _____

   _____

   _____

   _____

2. The idols in a child's heart that lead him (her) into rebellion are _____ and _____. (See page 55, last paragraph, in *The Power of a Praying Parent*.) Do you ever recognize either of those in your child? If so, write out a prayer that they be broken in your child's personality. If no, write out a prayer that they do not gain a foothold in his (her) life.

   _____

   _____

   _____

   _____

3. The opposite of rebellion is _____.
    The first step of obedience for children is _____.
    (See page 56, third paragraph, in *The Power of a Praying Parent*.) What would you say is the opposite of pride?
    _____. The opposite of selfishness?
    _____. Using all four of your answers, write down a prayer asking God to put those qualities in your child.

    _____

    _____

    _____

    _____

4. List the reasons you want your child to be obedient. (See page 56, third paragraph, in *The Power of a Praying Parent*.)

    _____

    _____

    _____

    _____

5. Read Ephesians 6:10-13 and underline it in your Bible. Star verses 11 and 12. According to this scripture, are you in a battle with your children? _____. If not, against whom do you battle?

    _____

    _____

    _____

    _____

6. Read Nehemiah 9:26-27 and underline these verses in your Bible. According to them, what does God do with His rebellious children? _____.
   What happens when they turn to God?

   _____

   _____

   _____

   _____

   _____

7. Do you ever see a rebellious spirit rise up in your child? _____.
   If so, how does it manifest itself? _____.
   Does it ever intimidate you? _____. Why or why not?

   _____

   _____

   _____

   _____

   _____

8. Do you believe that God has given you "authority over all the power of the enemy," including rebellion? _____.
   Do you for any reason feel hesitant to stand against your child's enemy in prayer? _____. Why or why not?

   _____

   _____

   _____

   _____

9. Write out a proclamation declaring dominion over the enemy, saying that your child belongs to the Lord and no force of hell will be allowed to control him (her) with rebellion.

_____

_____

_____

_____

_____

10. Pray out loud the prayer on page 58 in *The Power of a Praying Parent.* Include specifics related to your child.

_____

_____

_____

_____

_____

WEEK SEVEN

Read Chapter 7: "Maintaining Good Family Relationships"
from *The Power of a Praying Parent*

1. Did you grow up with good, close family relationships?_____.
   Explain.

   _____

   _____

   _____

   _____

   _____

   _____

2. Do you have close family relationships now? _____.
   Explain.

   _____

   _____

   _____

   _____

   _____

   _____

3. Is there any family situation that is strained, fractured, or sev-
   ered? _____. Write out your answer
   as a prayer asking God to restore it.

   _____

   _____

   _____

   _____

4. Does your extended family or did your ancestors have a history
   of breached relationships? _____. Are there now
   or have there been people in your family who no longer speak
   to or see one another because of some kind of breakdown in
   their relationship? _____. Explain. How do
   you think that heritage might affect your child?

   _____

   _____

   _____

   _____

5. Read Romans 14:19 and underline it in your Bible. Are you
   willing to be the peacemaker in your family by praying for all
   damaged relationships to be restored? _____.
   Write to the Lord your commitment to that end.

   _____

   _____

   _____

   _____

6. Are you willing to take dominion over the plans of the enemy and pray that family relationships in your child's life will not be broken down? Write out your answers as a prayer below.

_____

_____

_____

_____

_____

7. List below the important relationships in your family which are especially crucial to your child's happiness. Write out a prayer that your son or daughter will have a lasting and loving relationship with each one of these people.

_____

_____

_____

_____

8. Do you encourage your child to have a strong relationship with other members of your family? _____. Do you believe that feeling loved and accepted by other family members is crucial to your child's peace and happiness? _____. How could you pray to that end?

_____

_____

_____

_____

9. Read 1 Peter 3:8-9 and underline these verses in your Bible. Write them out as a prayer over your child with regard to his (her) relationship with a specific family member.

_____

_____

_____

_____

_____

10. Pray out loud the prayer on page 64 in *The Power of a Praying Parent*. Include specifics about your family relationships.

_____

_____

_____

_____

_____

WEEK EIGHT

Read Chapter 8:
"Attracting Godly Friends and Role Models"
from *The Power of a Praying Parent*

1. Read Proverbs 12:26 and underline it in your Bible. In light of this scripture, how important is it that your child have good, godly friends? Why?

   _____

   _____

   _____

   _____

   _____

2. Is there anyone you consider to be a bad influence upon your child? Is there anyone who seems to bring out the worst in him (her)? Explain.

   _____

   _____

   _____

   _____

   _____

3. Read Proverbs 13:20 in your Bible and underline it. Do you feel your child has any friends who are foolish? If so, what could happen if he (she) continues to spend time with them? If not, write out a prayer asking God to keep your child away from foolish friends.

    _____

    _____

    _____

    _____

    _____

4. Do you feel your child has friends who are wise? _____.
    Write out a prayer for those relationships to be strengthened.

    _____

    _____

    _____

    _____

    _____

5. Read 2 Corinthians 6:14-18 and underline these verses in your Bible. Does your child have any close relationships with non-believers? _____. What does the Bible say about that? How could you pray for those relationships?

    _____

    _____

    _____

    _____

6. Is there any relationship that is troubling or upsetting to your child? _____. Explain. If you don't know, write out a prayer asking God to give you revelation about the cause of that strife and what to do about it.

    _____

    _____

    _____

    _____

    _____

7. Read Ephesians 4:31-32 and underline these verses in your Bible. Does your child easily forgive others? _____. In light of your answer, write out these verses as a prayer over your child.

    _____

    _____

    _____

    _____

8. Who are the people your child looks up to in his (her) life? _____. Are they godly role models? _____. Write out a prayer below asking God to either strengthen those relationships or bring new ones into his (her) life.

    _____

    _____

    _____

    _____

9. Read Matthew 5:44 and underline it in your Bible. Write it out below as a prayer over your child. For example, "I pray that (<u>name of child</u>) will love his (her) enemies…"

_____

_____

_____

_____

_____

10. Pray out loud the prayer on page 70 in *The Power of a Praying Parent.* Include specifics about your child's close friends and role models.

_____

_____

_____

_____

_____

WEEK NINE

Read Chapter 9:
"Developing a Hunger for the Things of God"
from *The Power of a Praying Parent*

1. What does having a healthy fear of God mean? (See page 73, the second paragraph, in *The Power of a Praying Parent*.)

    _____

    _____

    _____

    _____

    _____

    _____

2. What influences in your child's life are trying to draw his (her) attention away from the things of God?

    _____

    _____

    _____

    _____

    _____

    _____

3. Write out a prayer asking God to take away the desire for those things that compete with Him for your child's attention.

_____

_____

_____

_____

_____

4. What are some of the things you can do to teach, instruct, train, and encourage your child in the things of God? (See page 74 in *The Power of a Praying Parent* for suggestions, but include your own specifics as well.)

_____

_____

_____

_____

_____

5. Read Proverbs 10:27 and underline it in your Bible. In light of this scripture, what is the main reason you should pray for your child to reverence or fear God?

_____

_____

_____

_____

_____

6. When our children develop a hunger for the things of God, they will know that the things of God are _____.
   They will become _____
   and not _____. They will long for
   His _____, His _____,
   and His _____. They will _____
   _____ and live a _____
   _____. (See page 74 in *The Power of a Praying Parent*.)

7. Read Psalm 34:8-10 and underline these verses in your Bible. What is promised for those who trust, fear, and seek the Lord?

   _____

   _____

   _____

   _____

   _____

   _____

8. Write out Psalm 34:8-10 as a prayer for your child. For example, "Lord, I pray that (<u>name of child</u>) will taste and see that You are good…"

   _____

   _____

   _____

   _____

   _____

   _____

9. How do you feel about your child's heart for God at this stage
    in his (her) life? _____.
    If you would like to see your child have a greater hunger for the
    Lord, write out a prayer to that effect.

    _____

    _____

    _____

    _____

    _____

10. Pray out loud the prayer on pages 75-76 in *The Power of a Pray-
    ing Parent*. Include specifics about your child's relationship with
    God.

    _____

    _____

    _____

    _____

    _____

WEEK TEN

Read Chapter 10: "Being the Person God Created"
from *The Power of a Praying Parent*

1. Do you believe your child ever compares himself (herself) unfavorably to others? _____. How so?

   _____

   _____

   _____

   _____

   _____

   _____

2. Do you ever compare yourself unfavorably to others? _____.
   If so, how might your doing so affect your child's attitude about himself (herself)?

   _____

   _____

   _____

   _____

   _____

   _____

3. Do you ever see your child striving to be something he (she) was not created to be, or straining to do something that will never fulfill him (her)? _____. Describe that.

    _____

    _____

    _____

    _____

    _____

    _____

4. Write out a prayer asking God to reveal to your child the truth about who He created him (her) to be.

    _____

    _____

    _____

    _____

    _____

    _____

5. Write out a prayer asking God to reveal to you what your child's gifts and talents are. Write down what God shows you.

    _____

    _____

    _____

    _____

    _____

6. Write out a prayer asking God to reveal to you how to best nurture the gifts and talents He has placed in your child.

   _____

   _____

   _____

   _____

   _____

7. Read Isaiah 44:3-5 and underline these verses in your Bible. In verses 3 and 4, what are the rewards for the person who hungers and thirsts for more of the Lord? _____

   _____.

   How will your desire for more of the Lord affect your child?

   _____

   _____

   _____

   _____

   _____

8. In verse 5 of the above scripture, what will the children say that is foundational to knowing who they are?

   _____

   _____

   _____

   _____

   _____

9. Does your child know with certainty that he (she) belongs to the Lord? Write out your answer in a prayer asking God to make that a reality in his (her) mind.

_____

_____

_____

_____

_____

10. Pray out loud the prayer on pages 82-83 in *The Power of a Praying Parent.* Include specifics about your child.

_____

_____

_____

_____

_____

WEEK ELEVEN

Read Chapter 11: "Following Truth, Rejecting Lies"
from *The Power of a Praying Parent*

1. Read Proverbs 12:22 and underline it in your Bible. How does God feel about lying? _____
   _____. How does He feel about people who tell the truth? _____.

2. Read Proverbs 21:6 and underline it in your Bible. In light of this scripture, what is the main reason that we must teach our children not to lie?

   _____

   _____

   _____

   _____

3. Do you believe lying is a serious offense against God? _____.
   Explain how serious you think it is.

   _____

   _____

   _____

   _____

4. How do you believe your own attitude toward lying affects your child?

_____

_____

_____

_____

_____

_____

5. What could you say to communicate to your child the seriousness of telling lies and the rewards of telling the truth?

_____

_____

_____

_____

_____

6. Read John 14:15-17 and underline these verses in your Bible. Who is the Helper God gives us when we live His way? _____. Write out a prayer asking God to pour out His Spirit upon your child so that he (she) will receive the Spirit of truth.

_____

_____

_____

_____

_____

7. Read John 8:44 and underline it in your Bible. Who is the father of lies? _____. When your child tells a lie, with whom has he (she) aligned himself (herself)? _____. Write out a prayer asking God to help you teach your child the seriousness of aligning his or her heart with the father of lies.

_____

_____

_____

_____

_____

8. Do you feel that your child already has a problem with lying? _____. Are you concerned that a tendency to lie might develop in the future? _____. Write out a proclamation stating that your child's heart belongs to God and no part of it will be surrendered to the enemy, the father of lies.

_____

_____

_____

_____

9. Read Psalm 69:5 and underline it in your Bible. Write out a prayer asking God to reveal to you any time your child tells a lie, so that nothing will be hidden. Ask God to help you establish appropriate discipline when lying does occur, so that you will effectively communicate the seriousness of the offense.

_____

_____

_____

_____

10. Pray out loud the prayer on page 88 in *The Power of a Praying Parent*. Include specifics about your child's ability to follow truth and reject lies.

_____

_____

_____

_____

WEEK TWELVE

Read Chapter 12: "Enjoying a Life of Health and Healing"
from *The Power of a Praying Parent*

1. Read James 5:15-16 and underline these verses in your Bible.
   Put a star next to each verse. What does this scripture tell you to
   do if you or your child is sick? _____
   _____. What does God promise will hap-
   pen when you do that?

   _____

   _____

   _____

   _____

   _____

2. Read Matthew 8:16-17 and underline these verses in your Bible.
   What did Isaiah prophesy that Jesus fulfilled?

   _____

   _____

   _____

   _____

   _____

Do you believe this is true for you and your child?

_____

_____

_____

_____

_____

3. Does your child suffer from any physical ailment? _____
    _____. Are you concerned about any particular
    sickness developing or injury happening? _____. Describe
    these and write how you could pray on an ongoing basis for
    your child about these concerns.

    _____

    _____

    _____

    _____

4. Have you ever prayed for healing for your child?_____.
    Do you believe that God answers prayers for healing through
    doctors and medicine, and to deny a child medical treatment
    when it is needed is wrong? _____. What are some
    of the answers to prayer for healing by miracles or medical treat-
    ment you have seen as a result of you or others praying?

    _____

    _____

    _____

    _____

5. Read 2 Corinthians 5:7 and underline it in your Bible. Are you willing to continue to pray and believe for healing even when you don't see healing happening right away? _____.
Why or why not?

_____

_____

_____

_____

_____

6. Read Acts 14:8-10 and underline these verses in your Bible. What was the key to this man's healing?

_____

_____

_____

_____

_____

7. When God looks upon you, does He see someone with faith enough to believe for healing? _____. Why or why not? _____

_____.

How would you like to pray about this?

_____

_____

_____

_____

8. Write out a prayer below asking God to increase your faith to believe for healing in the people for whom you pray.

_____

_____

_____

_____

_____

9. Write out a prayer asking God to give your child a faith strong enough to believe for God's healing power to flow on an ongoing basis through his (her) life.

_____

_____

_____

_____

_____

10. Pray out loud the prayer on page 94 in *The Power of a Praying Parent.* Include specifics about your child's health.

_____

_____

_____

_____

_____

WEEK THIRTEEN

Read Chapter 13:
"Having the Motivation for Proper Body Care"
from *The Power of a Praying Parent*

1. Have you ever struggled with poor eating or exercise habits, smoking, drinking, or any other kind of neglect or abuse of your physical body? Describe.

   _____

   _____

   _____

   _____

2. With regard to your previous answer, how different do you think you would be today if you'd had parents who prayed for you to have the discipline, self-control, and wisdom to be able to eat right, exercise regularly, and take good care of your body? Explain.

   _____

   _____

   _____

   _____

3. Read 1 Corinthians 6:19-20 in your Bible and underline these verses. What is the temple of the Holy Spirit? _____.
Do you believe it is important to see taking care of your temple as a ministry to God? _____. Explain why or why not.

_____

_____

_____

_____

_____

4. What is God saying to you personally through 1 Corinthians 6:19-20? If you are not certain, write out a prayer asking Him to show you.

_____

_____

_____

_____

_____

5. Write 1 Corinthians 6:19-20 as a prayer over yourself. ("Lord, I pray You will help me to remember that my body is…")

_____

_____

_____

_____

_____

6. Write 1 Corinthians 6:19-20 as a prayer over your child. For example, "Lord, I pray You will help (name of child) understand that his (her) body is…"

_____

_____

_____

_____

_____

7. Have you noticed any tendency in your child to abuse his (her) physical body or neglect to care for it properly? Write out a prayer about it and be specific.

_____

_____

_____

_____

8. Read 1 Corinthians 10:31 and underline it in your Bible. In light of this scripture, how should you pray for your child's attitude in regard to taking care of his (her) physical health?

_____

_____

_____

_____

9. Read 1 Corinthians 3:17 and underline it in your Bible. In light of this scripture, why is it important to pray for your child to take care of his (her) body?

_____

_____

_____

_____

_____

10. Pray out loud the prayer on pages 99-100 in *The Power of a Praying Parent*. Include specifics about your child. Pray it again over yourself if you feel the need to do so.

_____

_____

_____

_____

_____

WEEK FOURTEEN

Read Chapter 14: "Instilling the Desire to Learn"
from *The Power of a Praying Parent*

1. Read Proverbs 1:7 and underline it in your Bible. Where does knowledge begin? _____.
   What will your child become if he (she) refuses to learn? _____. Why is it important to teach your child to reverence God?

   _____

   _____

   _____

   _____

   _____

2. Read Proverbs 2:10-12 and underline these verses in your Bible. Describe why it is good to pray for wisdom for your child. Explain what could happen if you don't.

   _____

   _____

   _____

   _____

3. Read Proverbs 3:13-18 and underline these verses in your Bible. Why should you pray for your child to have wisdom? _____. List the rewards that wisdom brings, and circle each one in your Bible.

_____

_____

_____

_____

_____

4. Read Proverbs 3:21-24 and underline these verses in your Bible. What are the reasons you should pray for your child to have wisdom?

_____

_____

_____

_____

_____

5. Read Proverbs 2:1-5 and underline these verses in your Bible. Write them out as a prayer over your child. For example, "I pray that (name of child) will receive God's words and…"

_____

_____

_____

_____

_____

6. What have you observed about your child's *ability* to learn? Be specific.

_____

_____

_____

_____

_____

_____

7. What have you observed about your child's *desire* to learn? Be specific.

_____

_____

_____

_____

_____

_____

8. In light of your answers to questions 6 and 7, write out a prayer about your child. Ask God to show you what you can do to help him (her).

_____

_____

_____

_____

_____

9. Read Isaiah 54:13 and underline it in your Bible. Who is the ultimate teacher of your child? _____.
When God teaches your child, what does He promise to give him (her)?

_____

_____

_____

_____

_____

10. Pray out loud the prayer on page 105 in *The Power of a Praying Parent.* Include specifics about your child's ability or desire to learn.

_____

_____

_____

_____

_____

WEEK FIFTEEN

Read Chapter 15: "Identifying God-Given Gifts and Talents"
from *The Power of a Praying Parent*

1. Do you feel you have God-given gifts or talents that would
    have been better developed if you'd had someone praying con-
    sistently for you? How so?

    _____

    _____

    _____

    _____

    _____

2. Read Romans 11:29 and underline it in your Bible. Even if you
    feel your God-given gifts and talents have not been developed
    to the fullest, what does this scripture say about them? _____

    _____

    _____.

    What does that mean to you?

    _____

    _____

    _____

    _____

3. Do you observe any natural gifts, abilities, and talents in your child? If so, what are they?

_____

_____

_____

_____

_____

_____

4. Write out a prayer asking God to show you gifts and talents in your child that you have not seen before, or have seen but not with the clarity you would like.

_____

_____

_____

_____

_____

_____

5. Write out a prayer asking God to show you specifically how to best nurture, protect, and develop those talents and gifts God shows you.

_____

_____

_____

_____

6. Read Proverbs 18:16 and underline it in your Bible. Write out this scripture as a prayer for your child. For example, "Lord, I pray that the gifts and talents You have placed in (<u>name of child</u>) will make room…"

_____

_____

_____

_____

_____

7. Read 1 Corinthians 1:4-7 and underline these verses in your Bible. Write them below as a prayer for your child. For example, "Thank You, God, concerning (<u>name of child</u>), for that grace which was given to him (her) by Christ Jesus, that he (she) is being enriched in everything…"

_____

_____

_____

_____

8. Write out a prayer asking God to give you a glimpse of your child's potential for greatness. Include anything the Lord shows you.

_____

_____

_____

_____

9. Read Proverbs 22:29 and underline it in your Bible. Write out a prayer asking God to help your child excel in the gifts God has put in him (her), and for his (her) gifts to be recognized and appreciated by others.

_____

_____

_____

_____

_____

10. Pray out loud the prayer on page 110 in *The Power of a Praying Parent*. Include specifics about your child's gifts and talents.

_____

_____

_____

_____

WEEK SIXTEEN

Read Chapter 16: "Learning to Speak Life"
from *The Power of a Praying Parent*

1. Read Proverbs 13:3 and underline it in your Bible. Why should you pray about the things that come out of your child's mouth?

_____

_____

_____

_____

_____

_____

2. Words have power. We either can speak _____ or _____ into a situation. (See page 114, second paragraph, in *The Power of a Praying Parent*.) Who does it hurt the most when your child speaks words that are not godly?

_____

_____

_____

_____

_____

3. Have you ever heard your child speak ungodly words? _____.
    If yes, how did you handle it? _____
    _____. If no, how would you handle it
    if you did hear your child speak ungodly words?

    _____

    _____

    _____

    _____

    _____

4. Have you ever heard your child speak negative words about
    himself (herself)? _____. What did he (she) say and why
    do you believe those words were said?

    _____

    _____

    _____

    _____

5. Do you encourage your child to be open and honest about his
    (her) negative emotions and thoughts so you can pray with him
    (her) about them? _____. If your answer is yes, explain how
    you do that. If your answer is no, explain what you could do to
    encourage more open sharing.

    _____

    _____

    _____

    _____

6. Read Matthew 12:34-35 and underline these verses in your Bible. In light of them, how could you pray for your child's heart?

_____

_____

_____

_____

_____

7. Read Matthew 12:36-37 and underline these verses in your Bible. In light of them, why should you pray for your child to speak godly words?

_____

_____

_____

_____

8. Read Psalm 19:14 and underline it in your Bible. Pray this scripture as a prayer over your child. For example, "Let the words of my child's mouth and the…"

_____

_____

_____

_____

_____

9. A heart filled with _____, the truth
   of _____, and the _____ will
   produce godly speech that brings _____
   _____. This is where
   our point of _____ should begin. (See page 115
   in *The Power of a Praying Parent*.)

   _____

   _____

   _____

   _____

   _____

10. Pray out loud the prayer on page 116 in *The Power of a Praying
    Parent*. Include specifics about your child's speech.

   _____

   _____

   _____

   _____

   _____

WEEK SEVENTEEN

Read Chapter 17: "Staying Attracted to Holiness and Purity"
from *The Power of a Praying Parent*

1. Read Proverbs 20:11 and underline it in your Bible. What do you want your child to be known for?

    _____

    _____

    _____

    _____

    _____

    _____

2. Do you feel you are a good role model for your child as far as being someone who is attracted to holiness and purity?_____.
    How would you like to see that improve in your life?

    _____

    _____

    _____

    _____

    _____

3. Who is the real teacher of holiness and purity for your child?
    _____. Holiness begins with a love for
    _____. (See page 119, first paragraph, in *The
    Power of a Praying Parent*.) In light of that, how could you pray
    for your child?

    _____

    _____

    _____

4. The Bible says to "keep yourself pure," and that can only be
    accomplished by total _____,
    and the enabling _____.
    (See page 119, first paragraph, in *The Power of a Praying Parent*.)
    Write out a prayer about this for your child.

    _____

    _____

    _____

    _____

5. In order for your child to be attracted to holiness and purity, he
    (she) needs to see holiness and purity as attractive. Are there any
    people in your child's life who model that well? If so, write out a
    prayer for them to influence your child powerfully. If not, write
    out a prayer asking God to bring those kind of people into your
    child's life.

    _____

    _____

    _____

    _____

6. Read 1 Thessalonians 4:7-8 and underline these verses in your Bible. Who calls us to holiness? _____.
Who are we rejecting when we don't walk in holiness? _____
_____. Write out a prayer asking God to help you communicate this to your child in a way he (she) can understand and receive.

_____

_____

_____

_____

7. Read 1 Timothy 4:12 and underline it in your Bible. Write out this verse as a prayer over your child. For example, "Lord, I pray that no one will despise the youth of (<u>name of child</u>), but that he (she) will…"

_____

_____

_____

_____

8. Read Matthew 5:8 and underline it in your Bible. What kind of person is blessed? _____.
What is the blessing that person will receive? _____
_____. In light of this scripture, how could you pray for your child?

_____

_____

_____

_____

9. Read Psalm 24:3-5 and underline these verses in your Bible. Write them out as a prayer over your child. For example, "I pray that (<u>name of child</u>) will ascend into the hill of the Lord and…"

_____

_____

_____

_____

_____

10. Pray out loud the prayer on page 122 in *The Power of a Praying Parent*. Include specifics about your child's attitude toward living a holy and pure life.

_____

_____

_____

_____

_____

WEEK EIGHTEEN

Read Chapter 18: "Praying Through a Child's
Room" from *The Power of a Praying Parent*

1. Read Deuteronomy 7:26 and underline it in your Bible. Put a
   star next to this verse. Why do you have to be concerned about
   what is in your child's room?

   _____

   _____

   _____

   _____

   _____

2. Read Psalm 101:2-3 and underline these verses in your Bible.
   Write them out as a prayer over your child. For example, "Lord,
   I pray (<u>name of child</u>) will behave wisely and in a perfect way.
   I pray he (she) will walk within his (her) house with a perfect
   heart..."

   _____

   _____

   _____

   _____

   _____

3. Read Joshua 24:15 and underline it in your Bible. Put a star next to it. Write the last sentence out below as a proclamation.

_____

_____

_____

_____

_____

4. Write out the words, "As for me and my house, we will serve the Lord" (Joshua 24:15) on something and display it in your house. (My husband and I found a rock in our backyard, wrote this scripture on it with indelible ink, and set it on the hearth of our living room fireplace. Later, we put the rock right outside the front door. You could do something as simple as writing it on a piece of paper and posting it on the refrigerator door.) There is more power in doing this than you can imagine. Below, describe what you wrote the verse on and where you displayed it.

_____

_____

_____

_____

5. Does your child ever have nightmares, unexplained fears, or periods of aggressive behavior? _____. Explain.

_____

_____

_____

_____

6. Write out a prayer asking God to show you if there is anything unholy in your child's room, or anything that should not be in there. (For example, one of my friends prayed this prayer and God revealed to her that there was a stuffed animal in her young daughter's room that was scaring her and causing her to have nightmares. There didn't seem to be anything wrong with the stuffed animal, but it was not blessing this particular child. When she removed it, the nightmares stopped.)

_____

_____

_____

_____

7. Read Exodus 40:9 and underline it in your Bible. Have you ever anointed your child's room in that same way? _____. Why or why not?

_____

_____

_____

8. If you have never anointed your child's room and prayed over it, would you be willing to do so now? _____.Write out a prayer asking God to break every yoke of the enemy and cleanse your child's room of anything unholy. Then pray God's peace will always be in that room.

_____

_____

_____

_____

9. In what ways would you like to see your child's room become a
    sanctuary to him (her)? Explain.

    _____

    _____

    _____

    _____

10. Pray out loud the prayer on page 128 in *The Power of a Praying
    Parent*. Include specifics about your child's room.

    _____

    _____

    _____

    _____

WEEK NINETEEN

Read Chapter 19: "Enjoying Freedom from Fear"
from *The Power of a Praying Parent*

1. What are your fears? Explain.

   _____

   _____

   _____

   _____

2. Do any of your fears manifest themselves in your child in any
   way? _____. How so?

   _____

   _____

   _____

   _____

3. What are your child's fears that you are aware of at this point?

   _____

   _____

   _____

   _____

4. Ask your child what fears he (she) has and list them below. If it is not possible to ask your child that question, write a prayer asking the Lord to reveal to you any fears in your child. Be sure and write down whatever He reveals.

    _____

    _____

    _____

    _____

5. Have you ever noticed fear gripping your child's heart so that he (she) becomes unreasonable? According to Luke 10:19, over whom and what has Jesus given us authority? _____. Where does a spirit of fear come from? _____. Does it come from God? _____. Do you have the power and authority through Jesus Christ to resist a spirit of fear on your child's behalf? _____. Does fear have power over your child? _____. Do you have power over fear? _____. Can fear and the presence of the Lord coexist? _____. (See page 132, the last three paragraphs, in *The Power of a Praying Parent*.)

    _____

    _____

6. Read 1 John 4:18 and underline it in your Bible. In light of this scripture, how could you pray for your child with regard to fear?

    _____

    _____

    _____

    _____

7. Read Psalm 27:1 and underline it in your Bible. Write it out as a declaration of truth over your child. For example, "I pray for (<u>name of child</u>) that You, Lord, will be his (her) light and salvation…"

_____

_____

_____

_____

_____

8. Read Psalm 91:4-6 and underline these verses in your Bible. Put a star next to each verse. Write them out as a prayer to speak over your child. For example, "Lord, I pray You would cover (<u>name of child</u>) with Your feathers and underneath Your wings may he (she)…" Speak this over your child whenever he (she) is afraid.

_____

_____

_____

_____

9. Read Psalm 27:1 and underline it in your Bible. Have you ever noticed your child fearing the opinions of others? _____ . Why should he (she) not fear what others think about him (her)?

_____

_____

_____

10. Pray out loud the prayer on page 133 in *The Power of a Praying Parent.* Include specifics about your child's fears.

_____

_____

_____

_____

_____

WEEK TWENTY

Read Chapter 20: "Receiving a Sound Mind"
from *The Power of a Praying Parent*

1. Does your child ever struggle with confusion, the inability to stay focused, difficulty understanding things appropriate for his (her) age, or negative thinking? _____. Describe what you have observed.

   _____

   _____

   _____

   _____

   _____

2. Do you have any concerns or fears about the development of your child's mind? _____. What are they?

   _____

   _____.

   Why do you have those concerns?

   _____

   _____

   _____

   _____

3. Does your child have a tendency to be too self-focused? _____. Praising and focusing on God is the best way to combat self-centeredness. How could you pray about this for your child?

_____

_____

_____

_____

_____

4. Read Isaiah 26:3 and underline it in your Bible. Put a star next to it. According to this scripture, what should your child be focused on? _____.
   How could you pray about that?

_____

_____

_____

_____

5. Read Philippians 2:5 and underline it in your Bible. According to this scripture, how do we receive the mind of Christ? _____
   _____.
   Does it have to do with a choice we make? _____.
   How could you pray about this for your child?

_____

_____

_____

_____

6. Read 1 Corinthians 2:14-16 and underline these verses in your Bible. Can the natural man receive the things of the Spirit of God? _____. Why or why not? _____
   _____
   _____.

   When we receive Jesus and have the Holy Spirit in us, what do we have? (verse 16)

   _____

   _____

   _____

   _____

   _____

7. Read Romans 1:21 and underline it in your Bible. Bad things happened to these believers because they did not _____
   _____, and they were not _____
   _____. As a result, what were the bad things that happened to them? _____
   _____.

   Why should you pray for your child to have a heart that is thankful to God?

   _____

   _____

   _____

   _____

   _____

   _____

8. Read Romans 8:6 and underline it in your Bible. What kind of mind brings death? What kind of mind brings life and peace? What should you then pray for your child? Write out your answer as a prayer.

_____

_____

_____

_____

_____

9. Read 2 Timothy 1:7 and underline it in your Bible. Put a star next to it. Write this scripture as a proclamation over your child. For example, "God has not given (name of child) a spirit of fear…" Speak what you write out loud *to* or *over* your child.

_____

_____

_____

_____

_____

10. Pray out loud the prayer on page 137 in of *The Power of a Praying Parent*. Include specifics about your child.

_____

_____

_____

_____

_____

WEEK TWENTY-ONE

Read Chapter 21: "Inviting the Joy of the Lord"
from *The Power of a Praying Parent*

1. When you observe your child's face, does it most often reflect peace and joy, or is it frequently depressed, angry, sad, moody, or troubled? Describe.

   _____

   _____

   _____

   _____

   _____

2. Read Psalm 16:11 and underline it in your Bible. Where do we find joy? _____. Write out this scripture as a prayer over your child. For example, "Lord, I pray You will show (<u>name of child</u>) the path of life..."

   _____

   _____

   _____

   _____

   _____

3. Read Romans 15:13 and underline it in your Bible. Write out this verse as a prayer over your child. For example, "Lord, I pray that You, the God of hope, will fill (<u>name of child</u>) with all joy and peace…"

_____

_____

_____

_____

4. Read Psalm 118:24 and underline it in your Bible. Write out this scripture as a prayer over your child. For example, "Lord, I know that this is the day that You have made for (<u>name of child</u>). I pray that he (she) will…"

_____

_____

_____

_____

_____

5. Joy doesn't have to do with _____;
   it has to do with looking into _____and
   knowing _____. (See page 140, second to the last paragraph, in *The Power of a Praying Parent*.)

_____

_____

_____

_____

6. Read Galatians 5:22-23 and underline these verses in your Bible. Write out a prayer asking God to manifest each of these in your child. List each fruit of the Spirit specifically.

_____

_____

_____

_____

_____

7. Read Philippians 4:11 and underline it in your Bible. In light of this scripture, how could you pray for your child?

_____

_____

_____

_____

8. Read Proverbs 15:15 and underline it in your Bible. In light of this scripture, what happens to someone with a joyful attitude? _____. Write out a prayer about that for your child.

_____

_____

_____

_____

9. Read Numbers 6:24-26 and underline these verses in your Bible. Write them out as a prayer over your child. For example, "Lord, I pray You would bless (<u>name of child</u>) and keep him (her)…"

_____

_____

_____

_____

_____

10. Pray out loud the prayer on page 141 in *The Power of a Praying Parent*. Include specifics about your child's attitude.

_____

_____

_____

_____

_____

WEEK TWENTY-TWO

Read Chapter 22:
"Destroying an Inheritance of Family Bondage"
from *The Power of a Praying Parent*

1. Is there any trait, characteristic, or habit that you or your husband have which you would not like to see your child emulate or inherit? Write out your answer as a prayer asking God to keep that from happening.

   _____

   _____

   _____

   _____

2. Is there any negative tendency that seems to run in your family or your spouse's family that you would not like to see your child inherit (for instance, laziness, irresponsibility, self-pity, anger, unforgiveness, bitterness, gossiping, coldness, being critical)? Write out your answer as a prayer.

   _____

   _____

   _____

   _____

3. Are there any sinful or destructive patterns of behavior on either side of your child's family which you would not want to touch your child's life (alcoholism, infidelity, lying, unforgiveness, divorce, drugs)? Write out your answer as a prayer..

    _____

    _____

    _____

4. God has given you authority over all the power of the enemy. Take that authority and write out a prayer *breaking all the bondages* over your family that you listed in questions 1, 2, and 3. For example, "In the name of Jesus, I break the spirit of divorce, unforgiveness, and alcoholism, and I say that it has no part in my life or the life of my child…"

    _____

    _____

    _____

    _____

5. Read Romans 8:15-17 and underline these verses in your Bible. Whose child are you? _____.
    Where does your inheritance ultimately come from? _____
    _____. Where does your child's inheritance ultimately come from? _____.

    _____

    _____

    _____

    _____

6. Write out Romans 8:15-17 as a proclamation that your child's inheritance comes from the Lord.

   _____

   _____

   _____

   _____

   _____

7. Read 1 John 1:9 and underline it in your Bible. How do we become cleansed of the effects of sin? _____. Once we do that, what does God do? _____ _____. In light of that, how should you pray for your child?

   _____

   _____

   _____

   _____

   _____

8. Read Galatians 5:1 and underline it in your Bible. Write it out as a prayer over yourself and your child.

   _____

   _____

   _____

   _____

   _____

9. Read 2 Corinthians 5:17. Write out this scripture as a proclamation over your child, and then speak it out loud over your child. For example, "I say that (name of child) is a new creation…"

_____

_____

_____

_____

_____

10. Pray out loud the prayer on page 147 in *The Power of a Praying Parent.* Include specifics about your child.

_____

_____

_____

_____

WEEK TWENTY-THREE

Read Chapter 23:
"Avoiding Alcohol, Drugs, and Other Addictions"
from *The Power of a Praying Parent*

1. Read Proverbs 11:3 and underline it in your Bible. In light of
   this scripture, what would be a good character trait for your
   child to have in order to be able to resist any temptation that the
   enemy puts in his (her) path? Write out a prayer for your child
   regarding that.

   _____

   _____

   _____

   _____

2. One of the best ways to shield your child from temptation is to
   pray that he (she) be built up in the truth of the Lord. Write out
   a prayer to that effect for your child.

   _____

   _____

   _____

   _____

3. Read 1 John 4:2-4 and underline these verses in your Bible. How do you know that a spirit is of God? (verse 2) _____ _____. How do you know that a spirit is *not* of God? (verse 3) _____ _____. The Spirit in you is _____ _____ _____. (verse 4)

4. Do you believe you have authority over all the power of the enemy? (Luke 10:19) _____. Do you, then, have power over the enemy of your child? _____.Do you believe you have the power to break strongholds in your child's life through prayer? _____.Why or why not?

    _____

    _____

    _____

    _____

    _____

5. Read 1 Corinthians 10:13 and underline it in your Bible. Write it out as a prayer over your child. For example, "No temptation has overtaken (name of child) except such as is common to man…"

    _____

    _____

    _____

    _____

    _____

6. Read Romans 8:13 and underline it in your Bible. Write this as a prayer over your child. For example, "Lord, I pray that (<u>name of child</u>) will not live according to the flesh which brings death, but will…"

_____

_____

_____

_____

_____

7. Read Deuteronomy 30:19-20 and underline these verses in your Bible. In light of them, how important is it that your child make the right choices? What can happen if he (she) doesn't?

_____

_____

_____

_____

_____

8. In Deuteronomy 30:20, what three things must your child do in order to have a long life? _____

_____, _____,

and _____. Write out a prayer asking God to help your child learn to do those things.

_____

_____

_____

_____

9. Write out a prayer asking the Holy Spirit to help your child make right choices—choices for life—every day.

_____

_____

_____

_____

_____

10. Pray out loud the prayer on page 153 in *The Power of a Praying Parent*. Include specifics about your child's ability to resist temptation of any kind.

_____

_____

_____

_____

_____

TWENTY-FOUR

Read Chapter 24: "Rejecting Sexual Immorality"
from *The Power of a Praying Parent*

1. Read 1 Peter 2:11 and underline it in your Bible. Are the consequences of sexual sin manifested only in the body? _____.
   Where else in your child will there be damage from sexual sin?
   _____. From your own experience or the experience of others you know, can you think of an example where wholeness of the soul was sacrificed because of giving place to the lust of the flesh? Explain.

   _____

   _____

   _____

   _____

2. Read 1 Thessalonians 4:3-4. What is the will of God for our lives? What is the will of God for your child's life? Write out your answers as a prayer for your child.

   _____

   _____

   _____

   _____

3. Read Proverbs 28:26 and underline it in your Bible. In light of this scripture, how should we pray for our children?

_____

_____

_____

_____

_____

_____

4. Read James 1:12 and underline it in your Bible. Write out this verse as a prayer over your child's life. Remember that even if your child has already stumbled into sexual immorality, you can pray for him (her) to live in sexual purity from now on.

_____

_____

_____

_____

5. Are you convinced of the need for sexual purity in your life and the lives of your children? Write out your answer as a prayer asking God to show the consequences for sexual disobedience.

_____

_____

_____

_____

_____

6. Write out a prayer for yourself that you will never succumb to a trap of the enemy and fall into sexual immorality, including your thought life. (If there is any sexual immorality you have committed, speak a confession of it to the Lord so that the enemy has no grounds to have a place in your life.)

_____

_____

_____

_____

7. Read James 1:14-15 and underline these verses in your Bible. According to this section of scripture, how could your child be tempted? And what can happen if he (she) gives in to temptation?

_____

_____

_____

8. Read Galatians 5:16-21 and underline these verses in your Bible. How are we to walk? _____.
How are we not to walk?_____.
Write out a prayer listing the works of the flesh and pray that your child will avoid each one. Even a small child can manifest a seed that could grow into any one of these if it is not stamped out in prayer.

_____

_____

_____

_____

9. Read Galatians 5:22-23 and underline these verses in your Bible. Write out a prayer asking God to help your child exhibit every fruit of the Spirit mentioned here specifically.

_____

_____

_____

_____

10. Pray out loud the prayer on pages 157-158 in *The Power of a Praying Parent*. Include specifics about your child.

_____

_____

_____

_____

WEEK TWENTY-FIVE

Read Chapter 25: "Finding the Perfect Mate"
from *The Power of a Praying Parent*

1. Read Psalm 127:1 and underline it in your Bible. According to this scripture, why is it important that your child hears from God about who he (she) is to marry?

   _____

   _____

   _____

   _____

   _____

2. Read Proverbs 18:22. In light of this scripture, how does God view marriage? (Presumably what is true for a husband is true for a wife as well.)

   _____

   _____

   _____

   _____

   _____

3. Read 2 Corinthians 6:14 and underline it in your Bible. What kind of mate do you need to pray for your child to marry? _____. Write out a prayer for your child incorporating this scripture into it.

    _____

    _____

    _____

    _____

4. Read 1 John 1:7 and underline it in your Bible. In order for your child to have the kind of close relationship needed to make a marriage work, what does he (she) need to have in common with his (her) mate? _____. Write out a prayer to that effect.

    _____

    _____

    _____

    _____

5. Read Malachi 2:13-16 and underline verse 16 in your Bible. Why were the people crying at the altar of the Lord? _____

    _____.

    Why did God no longer accept their offering? _____

    _____.

    Why does He make a husband and wife to be one?_____.

    _____

    How does God feel about divorce and why?

    _____

    _____

_____

_____

6. Has there been divorce anywhere in your family? If so, write out
    a prayer asking God to break that spirit over your family. If not,
    ask God to keep it far from you.

    _____

    _____

    _____

    _____

    _____

7. The spirit of _____ keeps a mar-
    riage together. A spirit of _____ destroys
    a marriage. (See page 162, the fourth paragraph, in *The Power of
    a Praying Parent*.) Write out a prayer asking God to be in charge
    of your child's marriage, and that there be no divorce in his (her)
    future.

    _____

    _____

    _____

    _____

8. Write out a prayer that your child not only find the perfect
    mate, but that he (she) will not enter into marriage with expec-
    tations so high that his (her) spouse can't live up to them.

    _____

    _____

_____

_____

9. Read Colossians 1:9 and underline it in your Bible. Write out as a prayer over your child what Paul prayed here for the Colossians. Then pray for God to reveal His will to your child regarding his (her) future mate.

_____

_____

_____

_____

_____

10. Pray out loud the prayer on pages 163-164 in *The Power of a Praying Parent.* Include specifics about your child's future or present mate.

_____

_____

_____

_____

_____

WEEK TWENTY-SIX

Read Chapter 26: "Living Free of Unforgiveness"
from *The Power of a Praying Parent*

1. Does forgiveness flow freely in your family or does unforgiveness have a place in one or more family members? Explain.

   _____

   _____

   _____

   _____

   _____

2. Do you have any unforgiveness that you need to confess so you can be set free of it? If so, write out a prayer asking God to help you forgive. If not, write out a prayer asking God to reveal any hidden unforgiveness in you, and to keep you free from unforgiveness in the future.

   _____

   _____

   _____

   _____

   _____

3. Does your child find it easy to forgive or hard to let go of unforgiveness? Explain your observations.

_____

_____

_____

_____

_____

_____

4. Write a prayer asking God to show you any specific point of unforgiveness in your child. Then write down anything the Lord reveals.

_____

_____

_____

_____

_____

5. How could you pray specifically *with* your child about unforgiveness in his (her) life? Write it out as a prayer.

_____

_____

_____

_____

_____

6. Read Matthew 6:14-15 and underline these verses in your Bible. Why should you pray for your child to be a forgiving person?

    _____

    _____

    _____

    _____

    _____

7. Read Ephesians 4:31-32 and underline these verses in your Bible. Write them out as a prayer over your child. For example, "Lord, I pray that (<u>name of child</u>) will let all bitterness, wrath…"

    _____

    _____

    _____

    _____

    _____

8. Read 1 Corinthians 13:4-7 and underline these verses in your Bible. Write them out as a prayer over your child. For example, "Lord, I pray that (name of child) will have the kind of love that suffers long and is kind…"

    _____

    _____

    _____

    _____

    _____

9. Read Colossians 3:12-13 and underline these verses in your Bible. Write them out as a prayer over your child. For example, "Lord, I pray that (<u>name of child</u>), who is Your holy and beloved child, will put on tender mercies…"

    _____

    _____

    _____

    _____

    _____

10. Pray out loud the prayer on pages 170-171 in *The Power of a Praying Parent*. Include specifics about your child.

    _____

    _____

    _____

    _____

    _____

WEEK TWENTY-SEVEN

Read Chapter 27: "Walking in Repentance"
from *The Power of a Praying Parent*

1. Read Proverbs 28:13 and underline it in your Bible. What happens to someone who covers up his (her) sin? _____
   _____. What should your child
   be encouraged to do instead and why?

   _____

   _____

   _____

   _____

   _____

2. Parents can usually recognize a look of guilt on a child's face.
   Have you ever seen that look on your child's face? Whether you
   have or not, write a prayer asking God to keep your child from
   ever becoming comfortable with concealing his (her) sins.

   _____

   _____

   _____

   _____

3. Read 1 John 3:21-22 and underline these verses in your Bible. If your child confesses his (her) sin, what will he (she) experience?

_____

_____

_____

_____

_____

4. Have you ever detected sin on your child's face before you discovered it in his (her) behavior? _____. Describe. Do you feel God revealed that to you?

_____

_____

_____

_____

_____

5. Read Psalm 69:5 and underline it in your Bible. Even if your child can hide his (her) sins from you, can they be hidden from God? _____. Do you believe that when you pray, God will reveal your child's sins to you? _____.Why or why not?

_____

_____

_____

_____

6. Your child must be encouraged to admit or confess his (her) sin. But he (she) must also be repentant, or sorry enough to not want to do it again. Write out a prayer asking God to give your child a heart that is quick to confess sin and repent of it, and to seek forgiveness from God and others.

    _____

    _____

    _____

    _____

    _____

7. Do you think your child would be willing to pray such a prayer? Why or why not? How could you pray about that?

    _____

    _____

    _____

    _____

    _____

8. Read Psalm 139:23-24 and underline these verses in your Bible. Write them out as a prayer over your child.

    _____

    _____

    _____

    _____

    _____

9. Read Psalm 51:10-12 and underline these verses in your Bible.
    Write them out as a prayer over your child.

    _____

    _____

    _____

    _____

10. Pray out loud the prayer on page 175 in *The Power of a Praying
    Parent*. Include specifics about your child.

    _____

    _____

    _____

    _____

    _____

WEEK TWENTY-EIGHT

Read Chapter 28: "Breaking Down Ungodly Strongholds"
from *The Power of a Praying Parent*

1. Have you ever observed something in your child that you thought was not right, but you didn't have any hard evidence to support it? How did it manifest itself and what did you do about it?

   _____

   _____

   _____

   _____

   _____

   _____

2. Read Luke 12:2 and underline it in your Bible. How does this verse inspire you to pray for your child?

   _____

   _____

   _____

   _____

   _____

3. Write out a prayer asking God to always reveal to you the truth of what is going on in your child's mind and life.

_____

_____

_____

_____

_____

4. Do you ever see your child following a pattern of misbehavior (dishonesty, deception, greed, selfishness, arrogance, disobedience)? If so, describe what you see. If not, write a prayer asking God to reveal anything you should see.

_____

_____

_____

_____

_____

5. The devil always seeks to establish his rulership in our children's lives. Whether you see anything like that in your child or not, write out a prayer asking God to destroy any strongholds the enemy tries to establish in your child's life.

_____

_____

_____

_____

_____

6. Read Matthew 6:13 and underline it in your Bible. Write this scripture as a prayer over your child.

_____

_____

_____

_____

_____

7. You don't have to be suspicious of your _____, but you *do* have to be suspicious of _____ who is waiting to erect a _____ in his (her) life. (See page 179, last paragraph, in *The Power of a Praying Parent.*)

_____

_____

_____

_____

8. Read 1 Peter 5:8-9 and underline these verses in your Bible. What are you supposed to do when the devil seeks to attack your child?_____ _____. What is the best way you can think of to resist the devil's plans for your child?

_____

_____

_____

_____

9. What does the instruction to be sober, vigilant, and steadfast mean to you with regard to praying for your child to be protected from the enemy's plans? (See 1 Peter 5:8.)

_____

_____

_____

_____

_____

10. Pray out loud the prayer on page 180 in *The Power of a Praying Parent*. Include specifics about your child.

_____

_____

_____

_____

_____

WEEK TWENTY-NINE

Read Chapter 29: "Seeking Wisdom and Discernment"
from *The Power of a Praying Parent*

1. Read James 1:5 and underline it in your Bible. What is the promise to you in this verse?

   _____

   _____

   _____

   _____

   _____

2. Do you ever have concerns about your child's ability to make right choices and good decisions? Explain.

   _____

   _____

   _____

   _____

   _____

   _____

3. Do you believe you can ask God for wisdom for your child? Why or why not?

_____

_____

_____

_____

_____

_____

4. Read Proverbs 2:10-12 and underline these verses in your Bible. Write them out as a prayer over your child. For example, "Lord, I pray You will put wisdom in the heart of (<u>name of child</u>)…"

_____

_____

_____

_____

_____

_____

5. Read Proverbs 3:13-18 and underline these verses in your Bible. List below all the benefits of someone who has wisdom.

_____

_____

_____

_____

_____

6. Read Proverbs 4:7-9 and underline these verses in your Bible. According to them, what is the main thing we need? _____
_____. What else?
_____. What are the benefits of your child having wisdom and understanding?

_____

_____

_____

_____

_____

7. Read Proverbs 23:24-25 and underline these verses in your Bible. As a parent, what is the benefit for you if your child has wisdom?

_____

_____

_____

_____

_____

8. Read Proverbs 2:1-7 and underline these verses in your Bible. List the ways you can obtain wisdom and discernment. (For example, receive God's Word, treasure God's commands, etc.)

_____

_____

_____

_____

9. Write out Proverbs 2:1-7 as a prayer for your child. For example, "Lord, I pray (<u>name of child</u>) will receive Your Word and treasure Your commands within him (her). May he (she)…"

_____

_____

_____

_____

_____

10. Pray out loud the prayer on page 185 in *The Power of a Praying Parent*. Include specifics about your child.

_____

_____

_____

_____

_____

WEEK THIRTY

Read Chapter 30: "Growing in Faith"
from *The Power of a Praying Parent*

1. For his (her) age, do you feel your child has a strong faith, a weak faith, or somewhere in between? Explain.

_____

_____

_____

_____

_____

_____

2. Describe the kind of faith you would like to see your child have.

_____

_____

_____

_____

_____

_____

3. Does your child have self-motivation and a sense of purpose?
    Explain your answer.

    _____

    _____

    _____

    _____

    _____

    _____

4. Read Mark 9:23 and underline it in your Bible. Put a star next
    to this verse. Write the verse below. Take a moment to memo-
    rize it. At the first opporunity, teach it to your child and speak
    it whenever you can.

    _____

    _____

    _____

    _____

    _____

5. Sensing our limitations does not mean we have no _____
    _____. It's feeling that _____
    has limitations that indicates a _____.
    (See page 187, the third paragraph, in *The Power of a Praying
    Parent.*)

    _____

    _____

    _____

_____

_____

6. Children who have strong faith exhibit distinctly different characteristics from those who do not. Can you think of some of them? List them below. Does your child exhibit faith, or lack of faith, in any particular way? Explain.

_____

_____

_____

_____

_____

7. Read James 1:6-8 and underline these verses in your Bible. Describe what it is like for a doubter.

_____

_____

_____

_____

8. Read 1 Corinthians 13:13 and underline it in your Bible. What are the three things that will be lasting in your child's life? _____, _____, and _____. Write out a prayer asking God to give your child all three of these.

_____

_____

_____

_____

_____

9. Do you struggle with doubt or do you have a strong faith?
   _____. What kind of faith would you like to
   have? _____. Write out a prayer about
   this for yourself.

_____

_____

_____

_____

_____

10. Pray out loud the prayer on pages 191-192 in *The Power of a
    Praying Parent*. Include specifics about your child's faith.

_____

_____

_____

_____

WEEK THIRTY-ONE

Read Chapter 31:
"Getting Through the Teenage Years Successfully"
from *The Power of a Praying Parent*

1. Read Psalm 147:13. What is the promise for you and your children in this scripture?

   _____

   _____

   _____

   _____

   _____

   _____

   Write out a prayer thanking God for that promise and claiming it for your own children.

   _____

   _____

   _____

   _____

   _____

2. Read Proverbs 20:7. What does this scripture say about your part in your children's lives?

    _____

    _____

    _____

    _____

    _____

    _____

    Write out a prayer asking God to help you walk in such a way before Him that your children are blessed because of it.

    _____

    _____

    _____

    _____

    _____

3. Read Isaiah 54:13. What is the promise in this scripture regarding your children?

    _____

    _____

    _____

    _____

    _____

Write out a prayer asking God to make certain your children are taught by Him and not by anyone opposing His teaching. Claim the peace He has promised for your children.

_____

_____

_____

_____

_____

_____

4. Read 3 John 4. In light of this verse, do you think that what gives John joy also pleases God with regard to both you and your children? Why or why not?

_____

_____

_____

_____

Write out a prayer asking that your children will always walk in God's truth.

_____

_____

_____

_____

_____

5. Read Isaiah 49:25. What is the promise to you for your children in this scripture?

_____

_____

_____

_____

_____

_____

Write out a prayer thanking God for the promise contained in this verse.

_____

_____

_____

_____

_____

6. Read Isaiah 44:3. Write out a prayer thanking God for the promise to you and your children in this scripture.

_____

_____

_____

_____

_____

7. Read Psalm 138:8. What does this scripture speak to you regarding your concern for your children?

_____

_____

_____

_____

_____

_____

8. Read Deuteronomy 7:9. What is the promise for your children because you obey God?

_____

_____

_____

_____

_____

9. Read Deuteronomy 30:19. What does this verse say to you about the choices you make and how they will affect your children?

_____

_____

_____

_____

_____

Read Deuteronomy 30:6. What do you and your children need to do in order to live a good life?

_____

_____

_____

_____

_____

_____

Write out a prayer asking God to help you make choices for life, and choices to love God, so that your children will be blessed as a result.

_____

_____

_____

_____

_____

_____

10. Pray out loud the prayer on page 199 in *The Power of a Praying Parent.* Include specifics about your child.

_____

_____

_____

_____

_____

Answers to Prayer

*Be sure to record every answer to prayer you
receive for your child. You can start here, but
you are going to run out of room before long.
Remember, after you acknowledge what God
has done, be sure to thank Him for it.*

_____

_____

_____

_____

_____

_____

_____

_____

_____

_____

_____

_____

_____

_____

_____

Answers to Prayer

Answers to Prayer

Answers to Prayer

_____

_____

_____

_____

_____

_____

_____

_____

_____

_____

_____

_____

_____

_____

_____

_____

_____

Answers to Prayer

_____
_____
_____
_____
_____
_____
_____
_____
_____
_____
_____
_____
_____
_____
_____
_____
_____
_____
_____

Answers to Prayer

Answers to Prayer

_____

_____

_____

_____

_____

_____

_____

_____

_____

_____

_____

_____

_____

_____

_____

_____

_____

_____

Answers to Prayer

Answers to Prayer

_____

_____

_____

_____

_____

_____

_____

_____

_____

_____

_____

_____

_____

_____

_____

_____

_____

Answers to Prayer

Answers to Prayer

Books for Praying Parents
by Stormie Omartian

THE POWER OF A PRAYING® PARENT

Learn how to turn to the Lord and place every detail of your child's life in *His* hands by praying for such things as your child's safety, character development, peer pressure, friends, family relationships, and much more. Discover the joy of being part of God's work in your child's life. You don't have to be a perfect parent. You just need to be a praying parent.

THE POWER OF A PRAYING® PARENT BOOK OF PRAYERS

The Power of a Praying Parent Book of Prayers are a convenient way to draw your heart to the Lord in prayer. These prayers will give you confidence and peace in your parenting skills as you pray for God's best and most wonderful promises to come true in your children's lives.

THE POWER OF PRAYING® FOR YOUR ADULT CHILDREN

Stormie says, "Our concern for our children does not stop once they step out in the world and leave home. If anything, it increases. There is much more to be concerned about, but as parents we have less influence over their lives than ever. Even so, there is a way to make a big difference in their lives every day, and that is through prayer." This book by Stormie will help every parent to pray powerfully for their adult children and find peace in the process.

THE POWER OF PRAYING® FOR YOUR ADULT CHILDREN PRAYER AND STUDY GUIDE

The Power of Praying® for Your Adult Children Prayer and Study Guide offers special prayers and encouragement to lead you to lift up your adult children and specific areas of their lives, including faith and prayer life, family and relationships, direction and purpose, wisdom and integrity, and wholeness and healing.

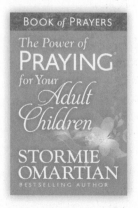

THE POWER OF PRAYING® FOR YOUR ADULT CHILDREN BOOK OF PRAYERS

This compact resource unveils the power of prayer to protect, nurture, and guide. It offers parents the comfort, reassurance, and wisdom of God's promises for them and their adult child's life and future.

Other Books by Stormie Omartian

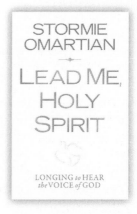

LEAD ME, HOLY SPIRIT

Stormie has written books on prayer that have helped millions of people talk to God. Now she focuses on the Holy Spirit and how He wants you to listen to His gentle leading when He speaks to your heart, soul, and spirit. He wants to help you enter into the relationship with God you yearn for and the wholeness and freedom He has for you. He wants to lead you into a better life than you could ever possibly live without Him.

PRAYER WARRIOR

Stormie says, "There is already a war going on around you, and you are in it whether you want to be or not. There is a spiritual war of good and evil—between God and His enemy—and God wants us to stand strong on His side, the side that wins. We win the war when we pray in power because prayer *is* the battle." This book will help you become a powerful prayer warrior who understands the path to victory.

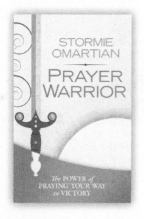

JUST ENOUGH LIGHT FOR THE STEP I'M ON

Anyone going through changes or difficult times will appreciate Stormie's honesty, candor, and advice based on the Word of God and her experiences in this book, which is perfect for the pressures of today's world. She covers such topics as "Surviving Disappointment," "Walking in the Midst of the Overwhelming," "Reaching for God's Hand in Time of Loss," and "Maintaining a Passion for the Present" so you can "Move into the Future God Has for You."

To learn more about Harvest House books and
to read sample chapters, visit our website:

www.harvesthousepublishers.com

HARVEST HOUSE PUBLISHERS
EUGENE, OREGON